Crossing Over

DR. MANUEL JOHNSON

Trilogy Christian Publishers
A Wholly Owned Subsidiary of Trinity Broadcasting Network
2442 Michelle Drive
Tustin, CA 92780

For information, address Trilogy Christian Publishing
Rights Department, 2442 Michelle Drive, Tustin, Ca 92780.
Trilogy Christian Publishing/ TBN and colophon are trademarks of Trinity Broadcasting Network.

For information about special discounts for bulk purchases, please contact Trilogy Christian Publishing.

Manufactured in the United States of America

10 9 8 7 6 5 4 3 2 1

Library of Congress Cataloging-in-Publication Data is available.

ISBN 978-1-64088-707-7 (Print Book)
ISBN 978-1-64088-708-4 (ebook)

CHAPTER 1

Crossing Over

We must understand that many of us do not cross over, and one of the biggest reasons is due to our hearts. We can say all the right things; however, our hearts are far from our tongue. Let us examine David, for instance. He was a man after God's own heart. But what was it about him that earned him the reputation of being a man after God's own heart. Throughout this book, we will closely examine the life of David, as well others, in order to answer this question.

The Bible mentions that in the day of Judges, Israel wanted to have a king, just as the other nations had. It says in 1 Samuel 8:4–5, "Then all the elders of Israel gathered together and came to Samuel at Ramah, and said to him, 'Look, you are old and your sons do not walk in your ways. Now make us a king to judge us like all the nations.'" Although this displeased the Lord and Prophet Samuel, the Lord gave them what they wanted. Similarly, He grants us what we want even when our hearts are hardened and are not focused on God's will. Hosea 13:9–11 states, "O Israel, you are destroyed, but your help is from Me. I will be your King; where is any other that he may save you in all your cities?

And your judges to whom you said, 'Give me a king and princes.' I gave you a king in My anger and took him away in My wrath." Psalm 106:12–15 states, "Then they believed His words; they sang His praise. They soon forgot His works; they did not wait for His counsel, but lusted exceedingly in the wilderness, and tested God in the desert. And He gave them their request but sent leanness into their soul." This is why we must examine ourselves to ensure that we are praying according to God's will and not our flesh.

In the book of 1 Samuel, we see that Samuel almost missed God's will when it came time to anoint a new king over Israel. Samuel initially looked at the outward appearance because Israel's first king, Saul, was chosen based on outward appearance and not the heart. First Samuel 16:6–7 states, "So it was, when they came, that he looked at Eliab and said, 'Surely the Lord's anointed is before Him!' But the Lord said to Samuel, 'Do not look at his appearance or at his physical stature, because I have refused him. For the Lord does not see as man sees; for man looks at the outward appearance, but the Lord looks at the heart.'"

First Samuel 10:9–10 states, "So it was, when he had turned his back to go from Samuel, that God gave him another heart; and all those signs came to pass that day. When they came there to the hill, there was a group of prophets to meet him; then the Spirit of God came upon him, and he prophesied among them." When Saul was under the anointing, he acted according to God's will; however, as soon as the anointing lifted, Saul's focus began to shift. Instead of focusing on establishing God's kingdom, Saul was focused on establishing his own kingdom.

"Now the word of the Lord came to Samuel, saying, 'I greatly regret that I have set up Saul as king, for he has turned back from following Me, and has not performed My commandments.' And it grieved Samuel, and he cried out to the Lord all night. So when Samuel rose early in the morning to meet Saul, it was told Samuel, saying, 'Saul went to Carmel, and indeed, he set up a monument for himself; and he has gone on around, passed by, and gone down to Gilgal.'" If, in our minds and hearts, we are striving to look good before man, we will never cross over to the Lord's perfect plan. Furthermore, we will constantly run into unnecessary problems with the Lord, just as King Saul did. We must always remember that every time we pray and have fellowship with the Lord, He examines our hearts, just as we read earlier in 1 Samuel 16:6–7.

See to it that you are not fooled due to the outward appearance, not just of people but of the things of this world. This can cause you to follow a path for years thinking that God is a part of it when He is not. Many times, Satan will put people or other things in your path to keep you from walking in the divine will of God. One of the keys to crossing over is to learn to hear the voice of the Lord. As we read earlier, when Eliab, Jesse's first son, was brought before Samuel, he was convinced through the eyes of his flesh that Eliab was the Lord's anointed. However, the Lord spoke to Prophet Samuel right then and there, and Samuel harkened to the voice of the Lord. Afterward, Samuel was not fooled by the appearance of Jesse's other sons, and he anointed the one who God had chosen.

When you hear and obey the Lord, He will anoint you to finish the job. Subsequently, your ability to hear God's voice will increase, just as it did with Prophet Samuel. "So Samuel grew, and the Lord was with him and let none of his words fall to the ground. And all Israel from Dan to Beersheba knew that Samuel had been established as a prophet of the Lord. Then the Lord appeared again in Shiloh. For the Lord revealed Himself to Samuel in Shiloh by the word of the Lord" (1 Samuel 3:19–21). Just as with Samuel, the Lord can establish you and reveal Himself to you.

CHAPTER 2

Personal Behavior

Let us revisit the story of young David to see how he was able to cross over to the heart of God. The Bible clearly tells us that we must behave appropriately at all times. Despite the envy King Saul had toward David, David conducted himself very wisely no matter what Saul tried to do to him. We must always remember that just because we can do something, it does not mean that we should do it.

David had not become king yet; he had not crossed over yet. Why? David had to endure a time of testing. There is a time of testing that we must also go through. We must remember that the Lord never stops furthering our growth in Him. As we allow Him to lead us and we obey His Word, we will, therefore, experience a tremendous growth of Christ in us. As previously stated, we must remember to behave wisely as David did. First Samuel 18:10–16 states:

> And it happened on the next day that the distressing spirit from God came upon Saul, and he prophesied inside the house. So David played music with his hand, as

at other times; but there was a spear in Saul's hand. And Saul cast the spear, for he said, "I will pin David to the wall!" But David escaped his presence twice. Now Saul was afraid of David, because the Lord was with him, but had departed from Saul. Therefore, Saul removed him from his presence, and made him his captain over a thousand; and he went out and came in before the people. And David behaved wisely in all his way, and the Lord was with him. Therefore, when Saul saw that he behaved very wisely, he was afraid of him. But all Israel and Judah loved David, because he went out and came in before them.

Similar to David, Joseph also had to endure a time of testing and processing. This time of testing did not stop after Joseph became governor. There were still seven years of plentiful to come as well as seven years of famine. In addition, he had to face his brothers who he hadn't seen in years. Genesis 42:6–10 states:

> Now Joseph was governor over the land; and it was he who sold to all the people of the land. And Joseph's brothers came and bowed down before him with their faces to the Earth. Joseph saw his brothers and recognized them, but he acted as a stranger to them and spoke roughly to them. Then he said to them, "Where do

> you come from?" And they said, "From
> the land of Canaan to buy food."
>
> So Joseph recognized his brothers,
> but they did not recognize him. Then
> Joseph remembered the dreams which
> he had dreamed about them, and said to
> them, "You are spies! You have come to
> see the nakedness of the land!" And they
> said to him, "No, my lord, but your ser-
> vants have come to buy food."

Many times, as the Lord raises us up the spiritual ladder, pride can come in and stop the flow of our spiritual growth. David made sure that he remained humble before God's people. First Samuel 18:5 states, "So David went out wherever Saul sent him, and behaved wisely. And Saul set him over the men of war, and he was accepted in the sight of all the people and also in the sight of Saul's servants." This does not mean that we will not face disappointment. As we cross over to the Lord's heart, we will face disappointment. Joseph was doing very well as a slave or head slave in Potiphar's house in the land of Egypt. The Lord was with Joseph, and He blessed Potiphar's house for the sake of Joseph. However, Potiphar's wife had other plans for Joseph. Yet Joseph would not yield to temptation and sin against the Lord. Genesis 39:7–10 states:

> And it came to pass after these things
> that his master's wife cast longing eyes on
> Joseph, and she said, "Lie with me." But
> he refused and said to his master's wife,
> "Look, my master does not know what
> is with me in the house, and he has com-
> mitted all that he has to my hand. There

is no one greater in the house than I, nor has he kept back anything from me but you, because you are his wife. How then can I do this great wickedness, and sin against God?" So it was, as she spoke to Joseph day by day, that he did not heed her, to lie with her or to be with her.

Similarly, David refused to lay his hand on God's anointed, King Saul. According to 1 Samuel 24:4–7:

Then the men of David said to him, "This is the day of which the Lord said to you, 'Behold, I will deliver your enemy into your hand, that you may do to him as it seems good to you.'" And David arose and secretly cut off a corner of Saul's robe. Now it happened afterward that David's heart troubled him because he had cut Saul's robe. And he said to his men, "The Lord forbid that I should do this thing to my master, the Lord's anointed, to stretch out my hand against him, seeing he is the anointed of the Lord." So David restrained his servants with these words, and did not allow them to rise against Saul.

Many times it seems as if we are repaid with evil when we try to do good. It happened with Joseph as well as David. When Joseph refused to lay with Potiphar's wife, he was sent to Jail. Also, David refused to lay his hand on King Saul, yet

Saul continued to pressure David until David allied with the Philistines for a season.

> And David said in his heart, "Now I shall perish someday by the hand of Saul. There is nothing better for me than that I should speedily escape to the land of the Philistines; and Saul will despair of me, to seek me anymore in any part of Israel. So I shall escape out of his hand." Then David arose and went over with the six hundred men who were with him to Achish the son of Maoch, King of Gath. So David dwelt with Achish at Gath, he and his men, each man with his household, and David with his two wives, Ahinoam the Jezreelitess, and Abigail the Carmelitess, Nabal's widow. And it was told Saul that David had fled to Gath; so he sought him no more.

We must not always look at a person's title or soon to be title. You want to make sure that you fit the title to which the Lord has called you to; that way, when the time comes, you are completely ready. This was the big mistake that Israel made. They wanted a king or, otherwise, a title. They wanted a physically appealing man with kingly features just like Saul. However, they never asked for a king who was after God's own heart. Prophet Samuel warned the people about the first king and what he would do them. Nevertheless, they cried out and claimed they wanted king regardless. This was displeasing to the Lord.

"Now, therefore, stand and see this great thing which the Lord will do before your eyes: is today not the wheat harvest? I will call to the Lord and He will send thunder and rain, that you may perceive and see that your wickedness is great, which you have done in the sight of the Lord, in asking a king for yourselves." So Samuel called to the Lord, and the Lord sent thunder and rain that day; and all the people greatly feared the Lord and Samuel. And all the people said to Samuel, "Pray for your servants to the Lord your God, that we may not die; for we have added to all our sins the evil of asking a king for ourselves."

God sent the thunder and the rain because he was displeased in Israel for asking for a king. Even after this, Israel still wanted a king just as the other nations. The nation of Israel was going backward, not forward, in their walk with the Lord. We must not go backward but cross over and go forward. When things appear to be evil, but you know that you are going toward the direction of God's will, stay focused, because it will all work out in the end. Romans 8:28 states, "And we know that all things work together for good to those who love God, to those who are called according to His purpose."

CHAPTER 3

Positive Influence and Forgiveness

Let us revisit the story of David and examine his character. An important point to remember is that we should never allow the people in our lives to influence us to partake in evil; even the people that God has put in our lives. At times, it can be easy to fall into this; however, that was not the case for David. At one point, David was living in a cave with six hundred men as well as women and children. It may seem that this situation was too overwhelming and that David had too much deal with; however, nothing is impossible with God (Luke 1:87).

During that time, David had to deal with troublemakers who tried to change the righteousness of David's heart. However, David overcame this and wouldn't allow them to influence him in a negative way. This showed us a true making of a king. David proved without a doubt that he crossed over. First Samuel 30:21–25 states:

> Now David came to the two hundred
> men who had been so weary that they

could not follow David, whom they also had made to stay at the Brook Besor. So they went out to meet David and to meet the people who *were* with him. And when David came near the people, he greeted them. Then all the wicked and worthless men of those who went with David answered and said, "Because they did not go with us, we will not give them *any* of the spoil that we have recovered, except for every man's wife and children, that they may lead *them* away and depart."

But David said, "My brethren, you shall not do so with what the LORD has given us, who has preserved us and delivered into our hand the troop that came against us. For who will heed you in this matter? But as his part *is* who goes down to the battle, so *shall* his part *be* who stays by the supplies; they shall share alike." So it was, from that day forward; he made it a statute and an ordinance for Israel to this day.

We can see that David is teaching the men a lesson. As the Lord gave them total victory and they recovered the spoils, David explained to the men that both jobs are important. The job of the men who went to battle with David is just as important as the jobs of the men who stayed to watch the supplies; both deserved to receive rewards. This idea was not in the minds of the wicked men who fought with David against the Amalekites.

Just as it happened to David, it will happen to you as well. At one point, you will find yourself in the middle of a situation where you have to make a righteous decision and do what is right in the eyes of God and not in the eyes of man. David was so firm on his decision that he declared an ordinance for all Israel when he became king. Therefore, it was not just David's idea; it was a God thing. While David was able to make righteous decisions without being swayed by the people, Saul was not able to do so. David even warned Saul about listening to the people.

According to 1 Samuel 24:8–9, "David also arose afterward, went out of the cave, and called out to Saul, saying, 'My lord the king!' And when Saul looked behind him, David stooped with his face to the Earth, and bowed down. And David said to Saul: 'Why do you listen to the words of men who say, "Indeed David seeks your harm?" And before this, King Saul even admitted and confessed his weakness of listening to the people.' Then Saul said to Samuel, 'I have sinned, for I have transgressed the commandment of the Lord and your words, because I feared the people and obeyed their voice.'" It is the Lord who should rule your heart and not people. Otherwise, you will never cross over to the heart of the Lord to where He wants you.

Someone who is seeking to cross over to the Lord's heart must have a forgiving spirit. This can only come from the Lord. You will be hurt many times in your life—by those you know and those you don't know, and by those who are close to you or far from you. Nevertheless, you must learn to forgive them by the strength of God. You must not seek revenge for revenge belongs to the Lord. This is made clear both in the Old and New Testament. "You shall not take vengeance, nor bear any grudge against the children of your people but you shall love your neighbor as yourself: I am the

Lord" (Leviticus 19:19). Furthermore, Romans 12:19 states, "Beloved, do not avenge yourselves, but rather give place to wrath; for it is written, 'Vengeance is Mine, I will repay,' says the Lord." You might be thinking, *But I have been really hurt!* However, no one has been hurt more than the Lord Jesus, and no one has forgiven more than Jesus.

The Lord has personally given me the strength to heal from deep wounds and to forgive all. He is faithful and will do the same for you if you ask Him every day and allow Him to heal you. This is very important in the eyes of the Lord in order to keep our record clean in His eyes regarding our past sins. Matthew 6:14–15 states, "For if you forgive men their trespasses, your heavenly Father will also forgive you. But if you do not forgive men their trespasses, neither will your Father forgive your trespasses." It is a commandment that we need to forgive as the Lord forgives us.

CHAPTER 4

Don't Judge Your Company

One of the problems that prevents us from crossing over is due to the fact that we tend to hang out with our personal cliques. We must look into our hearts and search to see if this is our doing or if it's from the Lord. When David was running from King Saul, David was around people who were distressed, in debt, and discontent.

> David, therefore, departed from there and escaped to the cave of Adullam. So when his brothers and all his father's house heard it, they went down there to meet him. And everyone who was in distress, everyone who was in debt, and everyone who was discontented gathered to him. So he became captain over them. And there were about four hundred men with him. These people, however, came

> to him from the Lord and he did not
> reject them. (1 Samuel 22:1–2)

Our Lord Jesus did the same thing; in fact, the religious leaders accused Jesus of keeping company with sinners, prostitutes, and tax collectors. "For John came neither eating or drinking, and they say, 'He has a demon.' The Son of Man came eating and drinking, and they say, 'Look, a glutton and a winebibber, a friend of tax collectors and sinners!' But wisdom is justified by her children" (Matthew 11:18–19). I am not suggesting that you hang out with people who do not want to change their life for the better; however, God will use you to be light to those who need help. At one point, you were walking in darkness until you allowed Jesus to come in and spiritually clean you. This is how the Lord used David. When David was running from Saul, he appointed the men who were with him as captains and officers.

> When he went to Ziklag, those of
> Manasseh who defected to him were
> Adnah, Jozabad, Jediael, Michael,
> Jozabad, Elihu, and Zillethai, captains of
> the thousands who were from Manasseh.
> And they helped David against the bands
> of raiders, for they were all mighty men
> of valor, and they were captains in the
> army. For at that time they came to
> David day by day to help him, until it
> was a great army, like the army of God.
> (1 Chronicles 12:20–22)

Therefore, you never know when the Lord will send people your way. Open up your heart and watch how the

Lord will increase your blessings. Recall how Jesus took uneducated fisherman and turned them into mighty men of God. The religious leaders even recognized it. "Now when they saw the boldness of Peter and John, and perceived that they were uneducated and untrained men, they marveled. And they realized that they had been with Jesus" (Acts 4:13). They gave the credit to Jesus. If Jesus did not give up on His disciples, then you should also be patient with those who the Lord sends to you. Also, do not judge; the Lord can send someone your way to be a blessing to you, perhaps even an angel. However, if you judge them by their looks, you can miss out on a great blessing.

According to scripture, we entertain angels unaware. "Let brotherly love continue. Do not forget to entertain strangers, for by so doing some have unwittingly entertained angels" (Hebrews 13:1–2). God will not just send people your way for ministry; it can be for all kinds of purposes. You may be a blessing to them, and in turn, they will become a blessing to others due to the experience they had with you. This is what happened with the disciples who stayed with Jesus until the end. He commanded to go and make disciples in His name. "And Jesus came and spoke to them, saying, 'All authority has been given to Me in heaven and on Earth. Go, therefore, and make disciples of all the nations, baptizing them in the name of the Father and of the Son and of the Holy Spirit'" (Matthew 28:18–19).

This was over two thousand years ago, and it is still continuing today. You can also have an impact like that if you will not judge and cross over to the eyes and the heart that the Lord wants to give you. Jesus warned us about judging. He said: "Judge not, that you be not judged. For with what judgment you judge, you will be judged; and with the measure you use, it will be measured back to you. And why do you look at the speck in your brother's eye, but do not consider the plank in your own eye" (Matthew 7:1–3)? If you judge others, you will not cross over and move forward. Instead, you will go backward.

Let us consider the story of Joseph. When God raised Joseph to power in Egypt, his brothers did an evil thing to him. Joseph could have had them killed, but he chose to forgive them rather than judge them. He made a clear statement asserting that he is not judge—only God is. Joseph had to cross over to where God wanted him.

So they sent messengers to Joseph, saying, "Before your father died he commanded, saying, 'Thus you shall say to Joseph: I beg you, please forgive the trespass of your brothers and their sin; for they did evil to you.' Now, please, forgive the trespass of the servants of the God of your father." And Joseph wept when they spoke to him. Then, his brothers also went and fell down before his face, and they said "Behold, we are your servants." Joseph said to them, "Do not be afraid, for am I in the place of God" (Genesis 50:16–21)?

It is important to watch your company and not judge!

CHAPTER 5

It's Time to Search our Hearts

So far, we've talked about looking at the exterior of a person. Now, let us focus on the interior. In Exodus 34:1, the Lord said to Moses, "Cut two tablets of stone like the first ones, and I will write one these tablets the words that were on the first tablets which you broke." The Lord wrote His commands and laws on tablets of stone to show Israel what their hearts were really like. The Lord actually wanted to write on Israel's heart and not on the stone, just as it is with us today.

It is important for us to read the Word of God daily, but it must be written in our hearts as well. This is what the Lord wants to do with all of us. He wants to change our hearts. He wants to write on our hearts His commands, laws, and His will for our lives. When we surrender ourselves to the Lord, He will also renew the Holy Spirit in us. We must allow this daily. "Then I will give them one heart, and I will put a new spirit within them, and take the stony heart out of their flesh, and give them a heart of flesh, that they may walk in My statutes and keep My judgments and do them; and they shall be My people, and I will be their God" (Ezekiel 11:19–20).

"But this is the covenant that I will make with the house of Israel after those days, says the Lord: I will put My law in their minds, and write it on their hearts; and I will be their God, and they shall be My people" (Jeremiah 31:33).

You might say, "This is just for Israel." No, if you are born again—that is if you have received salvation through Christ Jesus—then, you are under the same covenant.

Galatians 3:14 tells us "that the blessing of Abraham might come upon the Gentiles in Christ Jesus, that we might receive the promise of the Spirit through faith." This tells us that the Lord wants to write on our hearts. Paul even warns us not to harden our hearts toward the voice of the Lord.

> Therefore, as the Holy Spirit says: "Today, if you will hear His voice, do not harden your hearts as in the rebellion, in the day of trial in the wilderness, where your fathers tested Me, tried Me, and saw My works forty years. Therefore, I was angry with that generation, and said, 'They always go astray in their heart, and they have not known My ways.' So I swore in My wrath, 'They shall not enter My rest.'" Beware, brethren, lest there be in any of you an evil heart of unbelief in departing from the living God. (Hebrews 3:7–12)

Also, David expresses a similar warning in the book of Psalms.

"For He is our God, and we are the people of His pasture, and the sheep of His hand. Today, if you will hear His voice: 'Do not harden your hearts, as in the rebellion, as in the day of trial in the wilderness, when your fathers tested Me; they tried Me, though they saw My work. For forty years I was grieved with that generation, and said, 'It is a people who go astray in their hearts, and they do not know My ways'" (Psalm 95:7–10).

You may be asking yourself, "Why is this so important?" The world, as you can see, has hardened their hearts against the Holy Word of God. Prayer to the true God, Jesus Christ, has been taken out of homes, schools, workplaces, government places, and most of all, the hearts of men. The Bible even tells us that in the last days, the hearts of many will grow cold. "And because lawlessness will abound, the love of many will grow cold. But he who endures to the end shall be saved" (Matthew 24:12–13).

God doesn't want us to get caught up in this darkness that has been coming to this world. It is important that in these last days, we allow the Lord to write on our hearts. If you don't, Satan will take over your heart, just like what happened with Ananias and Sapphira. But Peter said, "Ananias, why has Satan filled your heart to lie to the Holy Spirit and keep back part of the price of the land for yourself? While it remained, was it not your own? And after it was sold, was it not in your own control? Why have you conceived this thing in your heart? You have not lied to men but to God" (Acts 5:3–4).

Do not think that just because there is a move of God happening, you are safe. There was a powerful move of God during the time of Acts, yet Satan still got into the hearts of people and caused death to many. You must guard your heart when you sense any signs of the devil trying to change you.

Do not be afraid. Just call on the name above all names—Jesus Christ. He will help you through the power of His Word and the Holy Spirit.

Let us recall how Jesus taught His disciples to pray. "Now it came to pass, as He was praying in a certain place, when He ceased, that one of His disciples said to Him, 'Lord, teach us to pray, as John also taught his disciples.' So He said to them, 'When you pray, say: Our Father in heaven, hallowed be Your name. Your kingdom come. Your will be done on Earth as it is in heaven. Give us day by day our daily bread. And forgive us our sins, for we also forgive everyone who is indebted to us. And do not lead us into temptation but deliver us from the evil one'" (Luke 11:1–4; see also Matthew 6:5–14). The disciples wanted to learn how to pray, and one of the things Jesus mentioned was, "Lead me not into temptation but deliver me from the evil one." What if Ananias and Sapphira would have prayed similar something similar to that with a pure heart? I believe the Lord would have delivered them from the hands of Satan.

God will always provide a plan of escape from temptation, but we must be willing to take it. "For in that He Himself has suffered, being tempted, He is able to aid those who are tempted" (Hebrews 2:18). Furthermore, 1 Corinthians 10:13 states that "no temptation has overtaken you except such as is common to man; but God is faithful, who will not allow you to be tempted beyond what you are able, but with the temptation will also make the way of escape, that you may be able to bear it." Therefore, if you allow the Holy Spirit to dwell in you and allow Him to change your heart daily to become Christ-like, then you and the people around you will see that there has been a true crossing over in you and in your heart.

CHAPTER 6

Heart Surgery

Let us take a closer look at the three main issues with the heart of man. Most of the time, we are hiding things in our hearts, even in the body of Christ. Many times, we don't realize that our heart is playing tricks on us. We must not get caught up in man's glory. What I mean is that just because you see person or a group of people performing great signs, wonders, and miracles, it doesn't necessarily mean that they are right with the Lord. We should never idolize a person or a group of people. We should also not idolize ourselves because it is the Lord who is working through us. "And God spoke all these words, saying: 'I am the LORD your God, who brought you out of the land of Egypt, out of the house of bondage. You shall have no other gods before Me'" (Exodus

Many years ago, I was taught as a minister that there are three important spiritual principles to abide by—they are referred to as the three Gs which stand for girls, gold, and glory. I was told to be cautious of girls (women), gold (money), and glory (this means to give all the credit and glory to God). Oftentimes, people will exalt men or ministers on a level they should never be on. This causes pride to come in their hearts and can cause them or their ministries to fall. The Bible tells us that pride comes before destruction. It also tells us that "everyone proud in heart is an abomination to the LORD; though they join forces, none will go unpunished" In the Old and New Testament, we have seen pride bring down men, both small and great. Let us take a look at the book of Daniel and examine what happened to King Nebuchadnezzar. The king had a dream about a very large, tall tree which had many branches and leaves. Many birds built their nests in that tree, and it could be seen to the ends of the Earth. Daniel interpreted the dream to King Nebuchadnezzar and told him that he was the tree and that the tree was cut down to its stump for seven years. This dream was a warning to King Nebuchadnezzar to repent and turn from his wicked ways and to live a righteous life before the Lord (see Daniel 4:19–26). However, the king did not heed the warning, and one year after the dream, King Nebuchadnezzar was again giving himself the glory. That very hour, the kingdom was taken from him for seven years.

Daniel 4:33 states "that very hour the word was fulfilled concerning Nebuchadnezzar; he was driven from men and ate grass like oxen; his body was wet with the dew of heaven till his hair had grown like eagles' feathers and his nails like birds' claws." After the seven years, King Nebuchadnezzar's kingdom was restored and so was his mind. He became a different man. King Nebuchadnezzar became humble. He realized that God was the ultimate king of kings, not him. He gave true glory to the God of creation, the living God, the God of Abraham, Isaac, and Jacob (see Daniel 4:34–36). Therefore, do not touch the glory.

In the book of Judges, there was a man named Samson who, by birth, was a Nazirite. Samson had a weakness with regard to women. He loved women, and it cost him plenty.

He lost his eyesight and his anointing of supernatural strength which the Lord gave him to subdue the enemy. Eventually, he also lost his life. However, Samson cried out to the Lord one last time, and God had mercy on Samson and gave him one more chance to have victory over the Philistines. "Then Samson called to the LORD, saying, "O Lord GOD, remember me, I pray! Strengthen me, I pray, just this once, O God, that I may with one blow take vengeance on the Philistines for my two eyes!" And Samson took hold of the two middle pillars which supported the temple, and he braced himself against them, one on his right and the other on his left. Then, Samson said, "Let me die with the Philistines!" And he pushed with all his might, and the temple fell on the lords and all the people who were in it. So the dead that he killed at his death were more than he had killed in his life. And his brothers and all his father's household came down and took him and brought him up and buried him between Zorah and Eshtaol in the tomb of his father Manoah. He had judged Israel twenty years" (Judges

Let us recall what happened to Ananias and Sapphira. As mentioned in previous chapters, they held back in their offering. Let us examine what God says about holding back that which belongs to God. Malachi 3:8–9 states, "Will a man rob God? Yet you have robbed Me! But you say, 'In what way have we robbed You?' In tithes and offerings. You are cursed with a curse, for you have robbed Me..." This brings us back to the gold. Remember to be cautious of the three Gs: gold, glory, and girls. The same goes for women to be careful with guys, glory, and gold. If we keep our pride down and maintain our finances and relationships according to God's commandments, we will receive a great reward and blessing. Therefore, let us cross over to trusting the Lord with our finances and do not become greedy. Also, trust the Lord for the man or woman he chooses for you till death do you part. And lastly, give the Lord all the glory and give Him thanks in all things (see Malachi 3:10–12, Proverbs 5:18–20, and Proverbs 3:5–6).

CHAPTER 7

Understanding the Will of God

When we cross over in understanding God's heart, we must learn that it is not about us. When we read the Bible, we see that it really touches the Lord's heart when we intercede for others and take upon the needs for others, not just for wages but in prayer time. In our time of prayer, we tend to focus on ourselves and our own needs. Many times, we get caught up in the worries of life which makes it harder for us to help others and intercede for them.

The kingdom of God is about serving each other and loving your neighbor as yourself (Leviticus 19:18). Let's take a look at Exodus 32:30–43.

> Now it came to pass on the next day that Moses said to the people, "You have committed a great sin. So now I will go up to the LORD; perhaps I can make atonement for your sin." Then Moses returned to the LORD and said, "Oh, these people have

committed a great sin, and have made for themselves a god of gold! Yet now, if You will forgive their sin—but if not, I pray, blot me out of Your book which You have written." And the LORD said to Moses, "Whoever has sinned against Me, I will blot him out of My book. Now therefore, go, lead the people to the place of which I have spoken to you. Behold, My angel shall go before you. Nevertheless, in the day when I visit for punishment, I will visit punishment upon them for their sin."

We see how Moses made a decision to return to the Lord after having spent forty days and nights with the Lord because Israel had sinned so greatly. This time, Moses spent forty days interceding for Israel. He prayed that God would remember the promise He made to Abraham, Isaac, and Jacob and that He would forgive the Israelites of their sins. Moses was willing to be taken out of the book of life for the sake of the Israelites because he loved his people. This is a person who has truly crossed over to the will of God; but Moses was being tested. In Exodus 32:7–14, we read that the Lord told Moses to leave Him alone. God wanted to wipe Israel out because they created a golden calf and sinned. Then, God offered to make of Moses a great nation. This was a big deal, and it could have caused anyone to get a big head. However, Moses remained humble. The Lord used Moses in a mighty way because he had a humble spirit and because he always prayed for Israel. Furthermore, the Lord allowed Moses to draw closer to Him and to learn more about who

He is. Moses was also able to see some of the glory of the Lord.

> So the LORD said to Moses, "I will also do this thing that you have spoken; for you have found grace in My sight, and I know you by name."
>
> And he said, "Please, show me Your glory."
>
> Then He said, "I will make all My goodness pass before you, and I will proclaim the name of the LORD before you. I will be gracious to whom I will be gracious, and I will have compassion on whom I will have compassion." But He said, "You cannot see My face; for no man shall see Me, and live." And the LORD said, "Here is a place by Me, and you shall stand on the rock. So it shall be, while My glory passes by, that I will put you in the cleft of the rock, and will cover you with My hand while I pass by. Then I will take away My hand, and you shall see My back; but My face shall not be seen. (Exodus

Moses showed God that it wasn't about him but that it was about accomplishing the will of God. Abraham carried the same spirit. He prayed for his nephew, Lot, who lived among the cities of Sodom and Gomorrah.

> Then the men turned away from there and went toward Sodom, but Abraham

still stood before the LORD. And Abraham came near and said, "Would You also destroy the righteous with the wicked? Suppose there were fifty righteous within the city; would You also destroy the place and not spare it for the fifty righteous that were in it? Far be it from You to do such a thing as this, to slay the righteous with the wicked, so that the righteous should be as the wicked; far be it from You! Shall not the Judge of all the Earth do right?"

So the LORD said, "If I find in Sodom fifty righteous within the city, then I will spare all the place for their sakes." (Genesis

Abraham interceded until he was at peace with the Lord regarding the righteous and the wicked. Due to Abraham's prayers, Lot and his daughters were spared from judgment.

And Abraham went early in the morning to the place where he had stood before the LORD. Then he looked toward Sodom and Gomorrah, and toward all the land of the plain; and he saw, and behold, the smoke of the land which went up like the smoke of a furnace. And it came to pass, when God destroyed the cities of the plain, that God remembered Abraham, and sent Lot out of the midst of the overthrow, when He overthrew the cities in which Lot had dwelt. (Genesis 19:27–29).

The Lord is looking for people who have a deep heart and spirit for others. God wants us to intercede, not just for people we know but also for people we don't know. Also, the Lord will put certain people on our hearts that we might never meet, and He will prompt us to pray for them.

Romans 13 tells us to respect and pray for governmental authorities. Therefore, it is not wise to speak against them. Second Peter 2:10–11 states, "And especially those who walk according to the flesh in the lust of uncleanness and despise authority. They are presumptuous, self-willed. They are not afraid to speak evil of dignitaries, whereas angels, who are greater in power and might, do not bring a reviling accusation against them before the Lord." Therefore, pray for your leaders. Also, it is important to note that it is a sin for leaders not to pray for their subjects. In Samuel 12:22–23, Samuel tells the people of Israel that he must pray for them; that it would be a sin against the Lord if he ceased praying for them.

God is also seeking those who would pray and intercede for the wicked. Isaiah 59:15–16 states, "So truth fails, and he who departs from evil makes himself a prey. Then the LORD saw it, and it displeased Him that there was no justice. He saw that there was no man, and wondered that there was no intercessor; therefore His own arm brought salvation for Him; and His own righteousness, it sustained Him." If we cease to pray and intercede, there could be a lot more judgment on this world, including on our friends and family. We ought to pray and intercede for our friends, family, and the nations.

And so it was, after the LORD had spoken these words to Job, that the LORD said to Eliphaz the Temanite, "My wrath is aroused against you and your two friends, for you have not spoken of Me what is right, as My servant Job has. Now, therefore, take for yourselves seven bulls and seven rams, go to My servant Job, and offer up for yourselves a burnt offering; and My servant Job shall pray for you. For I will accept him, lest I deal with you according to your folly; because you have not spoken of Me what is right, as My servant Job has." So Eliphaz the Temanite and Bildad the Shuhite and Zophar the Naamathite went and did as the LORD commanded them; for the LORD had accepted Job. (Job

After all that happened to Job, three of his four friends accused him of sin. They were not much help to him, yet Job still prayed for them, and the Lord's wrath was settled. If Job can do it, then, so can you. There is a great reward for those you pray for and forgive. This is a great cross over!

CHAPTER 8

Hearing the Voice of the Lord

In this chapter, we will focus on hearing from the Lord. There are many people who pray every day, but they do not or cannot hear the voice of the true and living God. There are many reasons for this; we will discuss some of the major reasons why the voice of the Lord cannot be heard. There are eight main reasons why you might not be able to hear from the Lord:

1. doing your personal will
2. distractions
3. praying to false gods
4. lack of prayer (having a prayerless life)
5. hardened heart
6. living in sin
7. unconfessed sin
8. always questioning the Holy Spirit or the divine plan of God

The Bible mentions these many times both in the Old and New Testament. Psalm 95:7–8 states, "For He is our God, and we are the people of His pasture, and the sheep of His hand. Today, if you will hear His voice: 'Do not harden your hearts, as in the rebellion, as in the day of trial in the wilderness.'" Paul also repeats this verse in Hebrews 3:7–8. Yes, the Holy Spirit does have a voice. However, the best way to hear the voice of the Lord is through His Holy Words— the Bible. If you question the Holy Words of God, then, you will probably question His voice too. God also speaks through dreams, visions, signs, and wonders, but He mostly speaks through His Word.

In the book of Numbers, the Lord spoke to Moses, Aaron, and Miriam, and He explained to them the various ways in which He speaks to people. "Then He said, 'Hear now My words: if there is a prophet among you, I, the LORD, make Myself known to him in a vision; I speak to him in a dream. Not so with My servant Moses; He is faithful in all My house. I speak with him face-to-face, even plainly, and not in dark sayings; and he sees the form of the LORD. Why then were you not afraid to speak against My servant Moses'" (Numbers

Furthermore, in the Old Testament, God would speak to His people with an ephod which the priest would wear over his chest (his heart). In the ephod was the Urim and the Thummim, and the Lord would direct the priest through the garment.

In the New Testament, we see that the Lord speaks through many dreams, visions, angels, and most of all, through the Holy Spirit. Matthew 2:19–21 shows how God speaks through dreams: "Now when Herod was dead, behold, an angel of the Lord appeared in a dream to Joseph in Egypt, saying, 'Arise, take the young Child and His mother, and go to the land of Israel, for those who sought the young Child's life are dead.' Then he arose, took the young Child and His mother, and came into the land of Israel."

In Acts 9:10–12, we see how the Lord speaks through visions: "Now there was a certain disciple at Damascus named Ananias; and to him the Lord said in a vision, 'Ananias.' And he said, 'Here I am, Lord.' So the Lord said to him, 'Arise and go to the street called Straight, and inquire at the house of Judas for one called Saul of Tarsus, for behold, he is praying. And in a vision, he has seen a man named Ananias coming in and putting his hand on him, so that he might receive his sight.'"

In Luke 1:26–29, we read how God can deliver a message through his angels. "Now, in the sixth month, the Angel Gabriel was sent by God to a city of Galilee named Nazareth, to a virgin betrothed to a man whose name was Joseph, of the house of David. The virgin's name was Mary. And having come in, the angel said to her, 'Rejoice, highly favored one, the Lord is with you; blessed are you among women!' But when she saw him, she was troubled at his saying, and considered what manner of greeting this was."

Also, God speaks to us through his Holy Spirit. Acts 13:2–3 states, "As they ministered to the Lord and fasted, the Holy Spirit said, 'Now separate to Me Barnabas and Saul for the work to which I have called them.' Then, having fasted and prayed, and laid hands on them, they sent them away." Most of all, the Lord speaks through His Word.

> So Philip ran to him, and heard him reading the prophet Isaiah, and said, "Do you understand what you are reading?"
> And he said, "How can I, unless someone guides me?" And he asked Philip

> to come up and sit with him. The place
> in the Scripture which he read was this:
> "He was led as a sheep to the slaughter;
> and as a lamb before its shearer is silent,
> so He opened not His mouth. In His
> humiliation His justice was taken away,
> and who will declare His generation? For
> His life is taken from the earth."
>
> So the eunuch answered Philip
> and said, "I ask you, of whom does the
> prophet say this, of himself or of some
> other man?" Then Philip opened his
> mouth, and beginning at this Scripture,
> preached Jesus to him. (Acts 8:34–35)

Jesus even said to His disciples that "heaven and Earth
will pass away, but My words will not pass away" (Matthew
24:35). Jesus also said for us to read the book of Psalms, the
prophets, and the laws of Moses as a witness of Him.

> Then He said to them, "These are the
> words which I spoke to you while I was
> still with you, that all things must be ful-
> filled which were written in the Law of
> Moses and the prophets and the Psalms
> concerning Me." And He opened their
> understanding, that they might com-
> prehend the Scriptures. Then He said
> to them, "Thus it is written, and thus
> it was necessary for the Christ to suffer
> and to rise from the dead the third day,
> and that repentance and remission of sins
> should be preached in His name to all

nations, beginning at Jerusalem." (Luke 24:44–45)

You don't ever want to come to a place where you can't hear the Lord's voice because your life will never be the same. This happened to King Saul; the Lord stopped talking to him, and he became a distressed king till his death. "When Saul saw the army of the Philistines, he was afraid, and his heart trembled greatly. And when Saul inquired of the LORD, the LORD did not answer him, either by dreams or by Urim or by the prophets" (1 Samuel 28:6)

Furthermore 1 Samuel 16:14–16 states, "But the Spirit of the LORD departed from Saul, and a distressing spirit from the LORD troubled him. And Saul's servants said to him, 'Surely, a distressing spirit from God is troubling you. Let our master now command your servants, who are before you, to seek out a man who is a skillful player on the harp. And it shall be that he will play it with his hand when the distressing spirit from God is upon you, and you shall be well.'"

The Bible clearly tells us that if you seek God, you will find Him. "Ask, and it will be given to you; seek, and you will find; knock, and it will be opened to you. For everyone who asks receives, and he who seeks finds, and to him who knocks it will be opened" (Matthew

Furthermore, we see Peter obeying the voice of the Lord in the book of Acts when he goes up to a roof to pray. "While Peter thought about the vision, the Spirit said to him, 'Behold, three men are seeking you. Arise, therefore, go down and go with them, doubting nothing; for I have sent them'" (Acts 10:19).

CHAPTER 9

By Faith and Not by Sight

The Word of God tells us that we must walk by faith and not by sight (2 Corinthians 5:10). This is how you can tell that you have truly grown in Christ, when you are no longer able to get away with doing things that you used to. What I mean is that there comes a time when the manna stops.

When the first generation of Israelites left Egypt, they walked and lived by sight and not by faith. They did not want to grow spiritually. Yes, there were many miracles in Egypt and in the wilderness; however, the Israelites were not victorious in their spiritual growth. Even with so many miracles, you can still harden your heart and miss the true blessing from God. You cannot cross over to the true promise of God unless you grow spiritually. You cannot put new wine in old wine skins (Mark 2:22). Jesus said, "Blessed are those who have not seen and believed." He never said blessed are the ones who see and believe. "And Thomas answered and said to Him, 'My Lord and my God!' Jesus said to him, 'Thomas, because you have seen Me, you have believed. Blessed are those who have not seen and yet have believed'"

The second generation of Israelites who left Egypt saw how their parents had hardened their heart toward the Lord's commandments and plans for them. They witnessed their parents' lack of faith. Now, it was their turn to show the Lord that they had faith and that they believed God's promises. Moses even warned them and told them what they must do once they enter the promised land. When they crossed the Jordan—and that generation was circumcised and kept the Passover—they ate of the produce of the land. After the Passover, the manna ceased to appear (See Joshua 5:8–12). This indicates that the second generation of Israelites began to walk by faith and not by sight. We must be able to see beyond our challenges through the eyes of the faith. This is what justifies you before the Lord. Romans 1:17 states, "For in it the righteousness of God is revealed from faith to faith; as it is written, 'The just shall live by faith.'"

Elisha knew he had to cross over to the Jordan; it would mean no more Elijah. He had to rely completely on the Lord. Previously, Elisha depended on Elijah. Crossing the Jordan also meant that the Spirit of the Lord would rest on Elisha but in different way—a double portion. Elisha had to grow spiritually to the point where he would be granted a double portion if he saw Elijah being taken up to heaven. "And so it was, when they had crossed over, that Elijah said to Elisha, 'Ask! What may I do for you, before I am taken away from you?' Elisha said, 'Please let a double portion of your spirit be upon me.' So he said, 'You have asked a hard thing. Nevertheless, if you see me when I am taken from you, it shall be so for you; but if not, it shall not be so'" (2 Kings 2:9–10). Not only did he receive a double portion from heaven, but he had the privilege of witnessing the heavenly chariots of fire in a whirlwind. When you are faithful, you not only receive spiritual growth but spiritual sight, which is far different from natural sight.

Nobody had the opportunity to see where Moses was buried; only the Lord and the angels knew. "Yet Michael the Archangel, in contending with the devil, when he disputed about the body of Moses, dared not bring against him a reviling accusation, but said, 'The Lord rebuke you'" (Jude 1:9)! So Moses, the servant of the Lord, died there in the land of Moab, opposite Beth-peor; but no one knows his grave to this day. Even the sons of the prophets did not have the opportunity to witness Elijah being taken up by the Lord.

> Now when the sons of the prophets who were from Jericho saw him, they said, "The spirit of Elijah rests on Elisha." And they came to him, they bowed to the ground before him. Then they said to him, "Look now, there are fifty strong men with your servants. Please let them go and search for your master, lest perhaps the Spirit of the Lord has taken him up and cast him upon some mountain or into some valley."
>
> And he said, "You shall not send anyone." But when they urged him till he was ashamed, he said, "Send them!" Therefore, they sent fifty men, and they searched for three days but did not find him, for he had stayed in Jericho, he said to them, "Did I not say to you, 'Do not go?'" (2 Kings 2:15–18)

This was a different level of anointing that Elisha was experiencing. He was experiencing not natural, but supernatural sight. This is why Elijah told Elisha, if you see me taken away to heaven, you'll receive a double portion. Why did Elijah say this? Only the Lord knows when we are ready for the next level of blessing. Elijah did not know whether Elisha was ready or not, he kept telling Elisha to wait there, but Elisha said, "No, I go where you go" (2 Kings 2:1–2, 4, 6). "And it came to pass, when the Lord was about to take up Elijah into heaven by a whirlwind, that Elijah went with Elisha from Gilgal. Then Elijah said to Elisha, 'Stay here, please, for the Lord has sent me on to Bethel.' But Elisha said, 'As the Lord lives, and as your soul lives, I will not leave you!' So they went down to Bethel" (2 Kings 2:1–2).

This shows that man does not chose the level of anointing in our lives, the Lord does. Are you ready to stop the manna in your life and cross over?

CHAPTER 10

It's a Test, Not a Challenge

Many times, as we are spiritually growing in the Lord, we do not know when it's the season of testing. This is chapter 10, which is the biblical number of divine testing. For example, we read in Numbers 14:1–25, that Israel refused to enter the land of Canaan because they believe the bad report of the ten spies regarding the giants in the land. This was the land that the Lord promised to Abraham, Isaac, and Jacob.

The Lord said that He would give this land to their descendants (Genesis 13:12–15). Abraham dwelled in the land of Canaan, and Lot dwelled in the plain and pitched his tent as far as Sodom. However, the men of Sodom were exceedingly wicked and sinful against the Lord. And the Lord said to Abraham after Lot separated from him, "Lift your eyes now and look from the place where you are, northward. For all the land which you see I give to you and your descendants forever." The Lord told Moses to send out twelve spies to spy out the land for forty days and to bring back a report. "Then Moses sent them to spy out the land of Canaan, and said to them, 'Go up this way into the south, and go up to the mountains, and see what the land is like: whether the people who dwell in it are strong or weak, few or many; whether the land they dwell in is good or bad; whether the cities they inhabit are like camps or strongholds; whether the land is rich or poor; and whether there are forests there or not. Be of good courage. And bring some of the fruit of the land.' Now the time was the season of the first ripe grapes" (Numbers

Ten out of twelve spies gave the children of Israel a bad report; this was the test of all tests for Israel. And the Lord said to Moses, "Because all these men who have seen My glory and the signs which I did in Egypt and in the wilderness, and have put Me to the test now these ten times, and have not heeded My voice, they certainly shall not see the land of which I swore to their fathers, nor shall any of those who rejected Me see it" (Numbers

If you have been walking with the Lord and have seen His power in your life from season to season, from year to year, then you are being tested too. You can pass the test; just believe in His Word and obey His voice. The number ten appears many times in the Bible in relation to God's testing. For example, in Malachi 3:10–11, the Bible speaks of the tithe, which is ten percent of your increase or your income. The Bible states that the tithe belongs to the Lord and that is ten percent (Numbers 18:21–24). Malachi also states that it is a test—we can test the Lord in our tithing and receive a supernatural blessing while doing so. However, Malachi also states that we are cursed with a curse if we hold back our tithes and offerings and that we have robbed God.

This is a test that you want to pass above all tests. If the Lord cannot trust you with just ten percent of your income, how can He trust you with anything else? How can you pass any other test?

Genesis 24:1–24 relates the story of Abraham who wanted to search for a wife for Isaac, the promised son. Abraham sent his highest servant, Eliezer, to go back to Mesopotamia to find a bride for Isaac. After months of traveling, Eliezer finally reaches Mesopotamia, and his camels were thirsty. Eliezer prayed and asked the Lord of heaven and Earth to give him favor. Eliezer asked the Lord that of all the women who came out to draw water from the well, whoever was willing to give him a cup of water and water his ten camels, she would be the bride for Isaac. A woman by the name of Rebecca came out, and she passed the test. Like Rebecca, what can the Lord test about you? Rebecca had no idea that the camels she was watering would be her camels and the servant she gave water to would become her servant. The story of your life can change. If you learn to pass the test and trust the Lord in all things, lean not on your own understanding and acknowledge Him, He will direct your paths (Proverbs 3:5–6).

Here are some basic tips:

1. Don't complain, proclaim in the Lord!
2. Don't be discouraged, be encouraged in the Lord.
3. Don't be faithless, be faithful in the Lord.
4. Don't give grudgingly, give cheerfully in the Lord.

CHAPTER 11

A True Relationship

I pray that after reading this chapter, the Holy Spirit will open your eyes to the true understanding of who Jesus Christ is. There are many people who are blessed by the hand of our Lord Jesus Christ but do not know Him or give Him the glory (Psalm 73: 1–19). Many times, we mistake someone's blessing, talents, special gifts, etc. as God loving them more than you and I; this is not so. And some of us believe people of different nationality and religious background are better because you see them prosper; however, in many cases, they do not want a relationship with the true living God Jesus Christ.

You can read any book you chose about Christ Jesus and still have a lost soul if Jesus Christ is not your Lord and Savior. Luke 16:19–31 tells us Lazarus was poor, and the other man was rich. Lazarus died, and the rich man died also, but Lazarus knew the true God Jehovah (Jesus Christ). No matter what you do in life, it's only the truth that makes you free (John 16:13–14). The Lord God, Jesus Christ, left His Holy Word for mankind to read, understand, believe, and follow as the Holy Word says, then, it will go well with you (Joshua 1:7–9).

The Holy Bible clearly tells us in both the Old Testament and New Testament that Jesus Christ is both Lord and Savior and the only true Messiah. Why would anyone want to prosper and still not be right with God. Some say who is the Lord that I should hear His voice or obey Him. The king of Egypt said this very thing (Exodus 5:2–3). The Lord has given us clear evidence in His Holy Word who Jesus Christ is and how He would be announced (Psalm 2:7). The Word of God tells us that:

1. Christ is the only begotten Son of God (Matthew 3: 17).
2. Christ will be resurrected from the grave (Psalm 16:10; Mark 16:6–7).
3. Christ will be scorned and ridiculed (Psalm 22:7–8 and Matthew 27:39–44).
4. Christ's hands and feet will be pierced (Psalm 22:16; John 20:25–27).
5. That others will gamble for Christ's clothes (Psalm 22:18; Matthew 27:35–36).
6. That not one of Christ's bones will be broken (Psalm 34:20; John 19:32–36).
7. That Christ would be given vinegar and gall mix, but He would not drink it (Psalm 69:21; Matthew 27:34).
8. That Christ would ascend to heaven (Psalm 68:18; Ephesians 4:8–9).
9. That Christ would be born of a virgin; Mary, the mother of Jesus knew no man (Isaiah 7:14; Matthew 1:18–23; Luke 1:34–36).

10. That there would be a forerunner for Jesus Christ (Isaiah 40:3–5 and Matthew 3:3).

11. That Christ would have a betrayer, and He would be paid thirty pieces of silver and would also break bread with Christ (Zechariah 11:12–14; Matthew 26:15–16; Matthew 27:9–10; Psalm 41:9–10; and John 13:18).

12. That Christ would first come riding on a donkey, a lowly colt (Zechariah 9:9–10 and Matthew 21:1–5).

13. Best of all, Christ is coming back soon, but this time in a glorious way, this time on a white horse with a powerful army of saints behind Him. You could be a part of this event if you know Jesus Christ as your personal Lord and Savior (Isaiah 11:4–5 and Revelation 19:11–16).

You may be thinking, *Why did Christ go through all that suffering?* Because of His love for you and for me. Christ paid the price He did not owe. Christ paid a price we could never pay. We could never pay it because we are born in sin. We have a sinful nature from birth (Psalm 51:5); Christ did not. He knew no sin, but we were conceived in sin. Our blood is polluted. Christ's blood is pure, and therefore he was the perfect sacrifice—the perfect atonement for our sins. John 3:16–18 states, "For God so loved the world, that He gave His only begotten Son, that whosoever believe in Him should not perish, but have eternal life. For God did not send His Son into the world to condemn the world; but that the world through Him might be saved. He who believes in Him is not condemned: but he who does not believe in Him is condemned already, because he has not believed in the name of the only begotten Son of God."

Why don't you—today, right now—make the Lord Jesus Christ your Lord and Savior, and you, right now, who have walked away from following the Lord come back to the Lord. Just call upon His mighty name right now.

Pray this: Lord Jesus Christ, received me back into Your kingdom and forgive me of my sins, put my name in Your book of life. I believe my sins are cleansed through your blood, I believe you are the Son of God, and You are the only way to everlasting life. Thank You for saving my soul. Amen!

CHAPTER 12

The Kingdom Business

You have read plenty of evidence leading to Jesus Christ. I believe the Lord has touched your heart. Now, it's time to be at the Lord's business. Most of the people in the world have their hearts set on their own business—their own glory—even to build a name for themselves. However, this Earth is going to fade away soon according to Isaiah 65:17, "For behold, I create new heavens and a new Earth; and the former shall not be remembered or come to mind." The Lord is going to do a total makeover on the Earth. John tells us he saw a new heaven and Earth. "Now I saw a new heaven and a new Earth, for the first heaven and the first Earth had passed away" (Revelation 21:1).

Also, there was no more sea. All these things we see on Earth and in space as we know as the second heaven will burn with fire. There will be a purification. "But the day of the Lord will come as a thief in the night, in which the heavens will pass away with a great noise, and the elements will melt with fervent heat; both the Earth and the works that are in it will be burned up. Therefore, since all these things will be dissolved, what manner of persons ought you to be in holy conduct and godliness, looking for and hastening the coming of the day of God, because of which the heavens will be dissolved, being on fire, and the elements will melt with fervent heat? Nevertheless we, according to His promise, look for new heavens and a new Earth in which righteousness dwells" (2 Peter 3:10–13).

Therefore, what you do here on Earth will not be credited to you unless you do it in the name of Jesus Christ. You will see your works into a form of a huge reward according to the Holy word of God (Matthew 25:34–46). "He who finds his life will lose it, and he who loses his life for My sake will find it. He who receives you receives Me, and he who receives Me receives Him who sent Me. He who receives a prophet in the name of a prophet shall receive a prophet reward. And he who receives a righteous man in the name of a righteous man shall receive a righteous man's reward. And whoever gives one of these little ones only a cup of cold water in the name of a disciple, assuredly, I say to you, he shall by no means lose his reward" (Matthew 10:39–42).

Even when Jesus was a young boy, about twelve years old, His earthly parents took Him to celebrate the yearly Passover, and after the Passover, they couldn't find little Jesus for a few days. When they searched for Him for three days, they found Him in the temple, with the priests, and He was about His heavenly Father's business (Luke 2:41–50). There was even a time when the disciples had asked Jesus how to pray, and the Lord gave them a foundation to start with. Jesus said "In this manner, therefore, pray: 'Our Father in heaven, hallowed be Your name, Your kingdom come. Your will be done, on Earth as it is in heaven. Give us this day our daily bread. And forgive our debts as we forgive our debtors, and lead us not into temptation, but deliver us from the evil one, for Yours is the kingdom. And Yours is the power. And Yours is the glory forever, amen'" (Matthew 6:9–13). This prayer is all about kingdom business, and this is just the foundation prayer. What would happen in your life if you shifted your mind and heart to the kingdom business—the powerful spiritual doors that the Lord would open for you.

This powerful attitude was in king Solomon's heart and mind in Kings 3:5–14. This was so pleasing to the Lord because at that time, it was truly in the heart and mind of King Solomon to do the right thing before the Lord. Solomon's mind and heart were on kingdom business—God's kingdom—and the Lord responded to Solomon and gave him the things he did not ask for such as long life, riches, and taking down his enemies. Even though he did not ask for riches, God gave him great wealth, which eventually became the downfall of King Solomon's kingdom. He raised up and exalted himself over God's will and kingdom.

When we exalt ourselves and build our own kingdom and give ourselves credit for what the Lord did, we will find ourselves outside of God's will and kingdom. Let us revisit the story of King Nebuchadnezzar.

> All this came upon King Nebuchadnezzar. At the end of the twelve months he was walking about the royal palace of Babylon. The king spoke saying, "Is not this great Babylon that I have built for a royal dwelling by my mighty power and for the honor of my majesty?"
>
> While the word was still in the king's mouth, a voice fell from heaven: "King Nebuchadnezzar, to you it is spo-

ken the kingdom has departed from you!
And they shall drive you from men, and
your dwelling shall be with the beasts of
the field. They shall make you eat grass
like oxen; and seven times shall pass over
you until you know that the Most High
rules in the kingdom of men, and gives it
to whomever He chooses."

That very hour the word was fulfilled concerning Nebuchadnezzar; he
was driven from men and ate grass like
oxen; his body was wet with the dew of
heaven till his hair had grown like eagles'
feathers and his nails like birds claws.
(Daniel 4:28–33)

Yes, King Nebuchadnezzar went too far, and the grace
of our Lord warned him to change his ways through Daniel.
"And inasmuch as they gave the command to leave the stump
and roots of the tree, your kingdom shall be assured to you
after you come to know that heaven rules. Therefore, O king,
let my advice be acceptable to you; break off your sins by
being righteous, and your iniquities by showing mercy to the
poor. Perhaps there may be a lengthening of your prosperity"
(Daniel 4:26–27). However, the king would not listen to the
good advice of Daniel. After seven years of total separation
from God and men and acting like a beast, the Lord restored
King Nebuchadnezzar's mind. As previously mentioned in
Chapter 6 of this book, King Nebuchadnezzar became a different person. He gave all glory to the Lord the Creator of
heaven and Earth, and he realized there is no other kingdom
that will last forever but the Lord's kingdom. "And at the end
of the time I, Nebuchadnezzar, lifted my eyes to heaven, and

my understanding returned to me; and I blessed the Most High and praised and honored Him who lives forever. For His dominion is an everlasting dominion, and His kingdom is from generation to generation" (Daniel 4:34).

So allow the Almighty God start to changing areas in your life that cannot be changed by men and totally put your trust in the Lord, in this world and the next.

A special prayer:

Thank You, Lord, for dying on the cross in my place and taking upon my sins. Thank You for being my Lord and Savior and keeping me focused on Your will, not mine. I'm looking forward to Your kingdom to come very soon. Lord, help me to be at my Heavenly Father's business every day till Your coming. In Jesus Christ's name, I pray. Amen!

Mega Praise Ministries
Pastor/Dr. Manuel C. Johnson
Final Remarks: December 1, 2019

It is my prayer that each and every one of you was truly blessed and inspired through the Holy Spirit in reading *Crossing Over*. Since the year 2000, the Lord began giving me predictions regarding political worldwide events such as America's presidencies, the first and second term election of presidents, and national economy.

Early 2001, the Lord revealed to me in a dream about two planes crashing into buildings. Also, He revealed to me that President George Bush Jr. would win a second term and that there would be an economy boom for a handful of years in America followed with a bad recession. In 2008, God revealed to me that Barack Obama would be our first black American president and that he would win a second term.

In 2016, the Lord revealed to me in a dream that Donald Trump would be the next president of the United States and that he would win a second term. In the first week of October 2018, on Mega Praise Ministries YouTube channel and also on Manuel Johnson's Facebook page, I made a public statement that Judge Kavanaugh would be confirmed and that Donald Trump would win a second term.

November of 2019, the Lord revealed to me that President Donald Trump would not be impeached. December of 2019, He revealed to me that Prime Minister Netanyahu would remain in office in spite of the allegations indictments pending. "Although I do not call myself a prophet, the Lord has been gracious to reveal to me these events" (Amos 3:7).

Sincerely,
Dr. Manuel C. Johnson

1 - (310) 295 - 0284

1158 26th Street

Suite 642

Santa Monica, CA 90403

megapraiseministries@gmail.com

6132

1 - 219 214 - 7316

CPSIA information can be obtained
at www.ICGtesting.com
Printed in the USA
BVHW040219260121
598763BV00019B/650

9 781640 887077